To my Mom & Dad, Emily and Bill Licate, who continue to support my journey every step of the way.

In loving memory of Grandma Carmel and Grandpa Sam, who taught me how to walk tall and love, unconditionally.

CONTENTS:

ACKNOWLEDGMENTS

My heartfelt gratitude goes out to my parents who bought me many pairs of shoes, made the publishing of this book possible, and who remain a constant support.

Many thanks to my family and friends who helped me discover pieces of myself, for inspiring me in their own unique way, and for including me in their lives and hearts.

A special thank you to Aunt Mary Frances Licate and Rosemary Timonere, for their boundless support.

A big hug to my beautiful editor, Cindy Pearlman, beautiful co-editor, Emily M.

Licate, and Authors, Judith Lukomski and Joseph Dispenza.

Love and gratitude to my companion animals. A special treat to my sweet rescue dog, Ollie, who sat on my lap while I wrote this book, and to The Brittany Foundation, www.brittanyfoundationonline.org, the wonderful dog rescue group that brought Ollie and me together.

THANK YOU

Mom and Dad, Grandma Licate, Aunt Mary Frances, Rosemary and James Timonere, Jamie Morrison, Raymond, Raechel, Jimmy and Janice Timonere, Little Jimmy, Jenna, Joy and Brother Bry, Juliann Rhodes and Danny, Amy Six, Julia Ruchman, Peter Zohos, Bill and Toula Zohos, Karyn de Dufour and Art, Jane and Clint Jackson, Sarah, Stuart, and Leggs, Uncle Jack and Aunt Florence, Toloria Milner, Jo Krasinski, Natasha Corbie, Wendy Gaunt and Nicole, Sarah Tarry, L. Stephanie Tait, Neil Dickens, Will Meyer, Justine Alessi, JayneAnn Colin, Dr. Kenneth Brace, Evie Kane, Karen Palmer, Judith Lukomski, Rebecca Allan and Laura Kaminsky, Linda Rich and Bob, Kim, and Brad, Aunt Patty and Uncle Tim, Colleen and Tim Allan, Matthew, Josh, Kathy Bryant and Rick, Barbara Smith-Antoline, The Ya-Ya's, Christopher Allan, Chris, Kurdt, Joseph Dispenza and Michael, Norma Jean and Ed Brady, Steven, Scott, Charity, Seth, Molly, and Sara, Almost Dad Royce Hayes, Dr. David Hurst Thomas and Lori Pendleton, Dr. James Adovasio, Frank

Baldwin, Christine Tarallo, Harrah's Girls, Courtney, Sue, Jen, Christina Van Oosten, Sarah Logan and James, Dick Houston, and Gypsy Gita.

Birds: Kali, Lucy, Ginger, Maryann, Dana, Tony, Michaela, Kate, Zoie, Grace, and Cara. Cats: Kim, Mani, and Curbie. Guinea Pig: Beth. Fish: Spaz. Hamster: Cubs. Dogs: Oliver, Claire, Misha, Deacon, and Smokey.

FINDING THE RIGHT FIT

Throughout life you grow and evolve. Sometimes you change enough where the relationships you have with places, people, and situations are outgrown or simply do not fit into the vision of your future. Like shoes that once fit you so well, relationships become too "small", out of "style", or just too "old."

I use the analogy of shoes because they escort you on your journey, every step of the way. If they get too small they can hold you back. If they get too tight and confining, they can cause discomfort. If they fit just right, they can help you move forward.

As you "step" through these pages, you'll explore the various changes in relationships

1

and find ways to embrace change for the better. Each chapter facilitates positive progress and offers opportunity for you to reinvent yourself. If you've always been someone who wears sneakers, break out and slide on a pair of patent leather dress shoes. In addition, I will share with you some personal stories that propelled me to grow.

Whether it is the evolution of your relationship with a friend, lover, family member, money, job, belief system or life style, inevitably, by being open and nonresistant, the changes taking place in your relationships can be your closest ally to self-fulfillment.

Finding the Right FiT

What you think you want most in the world may not be for your highest good. If something changes and falls away, let it, and in time you'll either get it back or realize that it wasn't meant for you. Something better will come along at the right time.

With love and light,
Camille

INTRODUCTION:
NOT MY STOP!

Life is about changing relationships. It's about relating in some way to every person, place, situation, or emotion. Some of these relationships stick forever and some are simply passing through. When change is afoot, in any relationship, it heralds opportunity for you to reshape your life.

There have been several occasions when I thought my life was finally "settled." I'd start a new job, meet a promising man, or move to a new location. In all these instances, I would envision my life and future, take a deep breath, and then hear three words in my head: "Not my stop!" Although my relationships to these situations, people, and circumstances all benefited me in some important way, in my core I knew that I had outgrown them. They were not the right fit.

It was time to give away the shoes I was wearing and go in search of a pair that would carry me on the next leg of my journey. Was it always easy? No! There were some shoes I carried with me for years until one day, I no longer had the space to pack them and take them along.

Change takes courage and you must constantly remember that throughout your life, change is inevitable. Moving forward demands leaving your comfortable space and

Introduction: Not My Stop!

sometimes starting again. There is the tendency to swim against the current of change and try ceaselessly to get back to that comfortable space. But, once back, it doesn't take long to realize that comfortable space is outgrown and therefore no longer satisfying. Imagine your favorite pair of shoes: one day they become so worn out that the padding is gone and the backsides begin to erode your heels. The shoes are taken off and replaced for a time. Once your heels are healed however, the favorite pair is worn once again. They are comfortable at first, but eventually begin to erode your heels once more, maybe this time to a greater degree. Now, you are forced to look back, bloodied heels and all, and wonder why you fought your way back to something that was no longer useful.

Small Shoes

Drawing from my life experiences, I can say that every change that has occurred, especially the ones I've cried over, has been to my benefit. I've learned change is *always* positive, even if it doesn't seem that way at the time.

For a number of years I was a professional ballet and modern dancer. My goal, since the age of seven, was to dance with a world-renowned company on a New York City stage. After years of dedication to my craft, I performed with the Martha Graham Dance Company at the Joyce Theatre in New York City. At the time, I was a scholarship student, but had high hopes of eventually being asked to join the company. However, one day I had a gut feeling that I needed a change. The dancer's lifestyle was no longer a right fit. Very clear about what I had to do, I forfeited my scholarship and retired from dance.

In the wake of this decision, I felt overwhelmed. I had just altered a lifestyle that I had been living for over eighteen years. However, I remained true to the flow of change in my life. I honestly believed I needed to follow a different path and accepted that I had outgrown the one I had traveled for so long. I looked back to my days with Graham with fond memories, but never with regrets. I truly surrendered to change, which was key.

A few months after making the decision to leave Graham, the Company made the cover of the New York Times, but it wasn't good news. I was astonished to read that the company had folded and the school had closed. Because I acted on the change I felt within, I was already traveling on my new path.

I have learned that life isn't about knowing it all. It's about continuing to be an active participant with its ebb and flow; knowing with every step, you are introduced to a new side of yourself.

1
RELATING TO YOUR *SELF*

The most important relationship you will have in your lifetime is with your *self*.

Look at what you are doing with your life. Are you giving out what you wish to get back or are you flip-flopping, wanting to stay in your "safe zone?" *Claim your heart's desire.* This will enable you to move forward.

Remember that, "progress comes *AFTER* rectification." If you see yourself in the same pattern, caught in the same web, in any of your relationships, at work, with family, friends, a lover, or with your thoughts, it is time to examine what is keeping you from growing and taking that step forward.

Small Shoes

Ask yourself, are you constantly regressing to familiar patterns even though you know the end result?

When you are willing to leave the familiar and make the necessary changes for advancement, it is like putting on a new pair of shoes and embarking on a new adventure. This can be unsettling because you cannot guarantee the new shoes will work, or, in other words, you cannot predict the outcome of a new venture. But, you can be guaranteed with change of choice comes change in experience!

There is no golden rule when it comes to your relationships. It's about knowing yourself well enough to know what is acceptable and unacceptable in your world. With this understanding, life becomes more about the joy of living than the trials of trying. It doesn't have to be an uphill battle in worn-out shoes. It can be a very pleasant hike, sometimes over craggy trails, but often with the feeling that you can soar over whatever is challenging you in the moment.

Time is an illusion, but timing is key. The choices you make at any given time are what feel right in that moment. Moments change and, therefore, choices change. In having sure-footed awareness, you can gauge how far you are willing to go for another person or situation. Once you make up your mind, the right relationships, under the right circumstances are delivered in proper timing.

Small Shoes

Gentle Reminder: Have patience with yourself. I find it so easy to have patience with others and sometimes difficult to have patience with myself. I feel as if everything must be immediate.

Everything has a right time. You are where you need to be.

2
RELATING TO FLOW: THE SECOND BUS

Have you ever been so inclined to toss all reason out the window and go with the flow? Animals and children are good teachers in the "flow department." They don't use logic to make their decisions. They simply do it! If something isn't working, they stop doing it. If they need something, they announce it with a cry, chirp, bark, or meow. I watch my little birds every day as they eat, play, nap, and preen. When the sun goes down, they get on their swing "in position" and grind their beaks in contentment.

How does this relate to going with the flow? Experienced, seasoned adults, have a tendency to stop the rightful flow of action with adult logic. There's the good old "what if" syndrome, the "I can't do that because so and so would never approve" or "I don't have enough money." If something is wrong, an adult finds some excuse to delay facing it; if one shoe is broken beyond repair, it is saved in a box thinking maybe one day it will be fixed. If you need something, you stay quiet. Why? *FEAR.*

What's the worst thing that could happen if you speak up, throw away, let go, and go with the flow?

One day a friend was driving me to the bus station. My bus left at 7 p.m., his car clock read 6:48 p.m. and we were in a traffic jam in a tunnel. He started to fret. I turned to him and said, "What's the worst thing that could happen?" He looked at me, his expression dropped back to a relaxed state, and he replied, "You'll catch the 7:30 p.m. bus."

BINGO.

The bottom line is there is always going to be a "7:30 bus." The Universe has many schedules, all of which are perpetually in service to accommodate you. There is a right time for everything, so where you are now, is exactly where you are supposed to be.

The battle is waged against yourself when you deny going with the flow. Life can be altered in a millisecond and all logical reasoning and planning is as useful as a wet match.

Why not embrace life's flow on both the minuscule and broadest of planes? Wouldn't that make living incredibly easier?

Small Shoes

Remember, a negative can turn into a positive just by shifting your perspective. So, go with the flow of your day, and at the end of it, grind your "beak" in contentment for the miracles, lessons, and joy you found along the way!

Gentle Reminder: If you are not accustomed to going with the flow, just practice. Like any new lesson, practice is the way to get better.

3
RELATING TO
YOUR CAREER

When I was a little girl, I wanted to be a Hula dancer. There was something so appealing about those long grass skirts and the fluidity of the Hula Dance. I did become a dancer, albeit with a focus on ballet and modern dance. I never wore a grass skirt, but did wear some amazing costumes and danced many wonderful dances.

My intention was to make a career out of dance. Then, my focus shifted, and I fell in love with acting, writing, and producing. I traded in my Pointe shoes for some flats, boots, and heels.

Small Shoes

You may be on a particular career path that leads you to the top of your field. Or, you may diverge, taking an entirely different path. Along the way, your chosen career, just like the style of shoes you wear, may begin to define you. You are a lawyer, farmer, doctor, or teacher. If and when your career changes in some way (you get laid off, you are relocated, the work no longer fulfills you) you must realize that it is *who* you are, not *what* you are that counts. The people that are meant to be in your life are not going to care if you are a custodian or CEO. You are you, no matter what!

Relating to Your Career

There is always room for change, just like there is room in your closet for new shoes. Whether you are in a career transition or you have a very fulfilling career, leave yourself opportunity to learn and grow. Wear a pair of shoes you wouldn't normally wear. If your work requires you to be inside most of the day, put on some riding boots and take a Horseback Riding lesson. If you are working outside the majority of the time, slip on some heels, go to a dance studio, and learn to Salsa. These new shoes may not lead you to a career as a horse-man or Salsa dancer, but they can offer you diversity in your chosen field or help you relax and unwind as you seek a new profession.

Small Shoes

As you grow and expand your horizons, you contribute to your current work and the work that is yet to come. And, who knows, maybe right now all you can imagine is working on Wall Street, with a busy firm, wearing your dress shoes, when actually, you will find your true happiness in your sneakers as a Dog Walker. You don't know where each step will lead. Just be sure, it will lead to the career that is meant for you!

Gentle Reminder: Love what you do, but love your life and the people in it more.

4
RELATING TO MONEY AND SUCCESS

Finally having money or your most coveted success doesn't necessarily spell out complete happiness. It's a wonderful accomplishment to gain financial security and to love your work, but your relationship to these fulfilled goals can't compare to the relationship you have with friends, family, your romantic partner, and yourself.

In the past, I've looked at people in certain jobs and felt sorry for them – especially if they looked tired or were underappreciated. I would feel guilty about my accomplishments and my successes, wishing that everyone could get a paycheck every week.

Small Shoes

If only these people made more money, lived in a better neighborhood, took a little vacation…

I changed my mindset when I worked for an extremely wealthy family in an affluent part of town. They had millions of dollars and every career success imaginable. Guess what? They were completely miserable and basically ignored each other while wailing about their collective boredom.

In contrast, I thought about a family I'd met when I visited a rural village in the rainforest of Borneo. This family had very few material goods, but amazing wealth. Their wealth had nothing to do with money. They spent a wealth of time with each other talking, laughing, telling stories, and guiding tourists, such as myself, through the lush rainforest. Upon returning from Borneo, I started to tell people that the greatest gift they could give me was their time.

Life, and your relationship with it, is not about having the "correct change." The cents or sense here is about living in integrity and leaving your positive footprint, whether you are wearing $400 Robert Clergerie wedges or $4 plastic sandals. It's who you are, not how much money you make that goes the distance!

Small Shoes

"I've learned that people will forget what you said, people will forget what you did, but people will never forget how you made them feel."

-Maya Angelou

Gentle Reminder: Cherish the simple things in life- the magnificent tree outside your window, the hummingbird at the feeder, the rain falling on the pavement. Give with both hands open and watch the wonders you receive!

5
RELATING TO EXPECTATIONS

I expected to see only pink blossoms,
But a gentle spring snow has fallen
And the cherry trees are wearing white coats.

-Ryokan (1758-1831)

To forgo expectations means giving yourself the opportunity to truly enjoy the life you are living **now**.

In contemporary society, there is pressure to be someone, do something, and possess as much material wealth as possible. You expect your life to take certain turns. Then a twist of fate turns you around and you're thrown off course. By expecting, you are outlining your life before you live it. "By the time I'm 30, I'll be _____ (fill in the blank with your own expectation).

Will you be married, have your dream home, or your dream job?

Who is to say if you're going to be able to fill in the blanks with exactly what you want on your exact timetable. The point is you shouldn't really try. When there is so much anticipation put on future events, there is little room to live in the moment and experience change.

When you expect a certain outcome, you are basing that expectation on your feelings and wants at that given moment. Circumstances change, relationships shift, and your view of what you want from life is oftentimes altered. This is not to say you're not to hope, dream, or set goals. Please re-read the Ryokan quote again and understand that life has its own way of reprogramming itself.

Looking back on a cherished time in your life, you may expect everything to stay the same. Once, I went hiking on a spring day in a magnificent canyon. I discovered a magical little area brimming with fern and ivy, tall leafy trees, and sunlit boulders. It was truly beautiful and I stopped to enjoy this lovely place.

A few months later when I returned to the same canyon, I hiked with great anticipation to this same place, expecting it to be the exact paradise retreat. It was completely different. In fact, the entire area had shifted with the oncoming winter season. The fern and ivy were a dusty brown and the trees were bare. Without the warm summer sun beaming, the grey and brown boulders sat cold and barren, almost blending into the colorless ground.

The tranquil setting this place had offered me in the past was not only visually and energetically different, but a bunch of little boys were playing on the rocks nearby, so the silence was broken with fits of loud screaming and laughter.

I felt disappointed because I had expected one thing and received another. As a result, my hiking and meditation plans needed to be rearranged. I left the area and found a small outcropping further into the canyon. I sat atop this precipice, eye level with the treetops, and felt the breeze in my hair and the sun on my face. It struck me how amazing it was that what I expected to find had changed and brought me to this new place, which was another wonderful discovery.

Without expectations, you allow miracles to occur in your life because you remain open to life's surprises!

Gentle Reminder: Let life be a surprise and then it will surprise you back, often, as they say, when you least expect it!

6
RELATING TO SURRENDER

How do you live a life without expectations? Surrender.

In other words, let go. Let life happen.

Surrendering is actually a lot easier than it seems. If you try on a pair of shoes and there is a spot that pinches your toe, you put them back in the box and let them go. This is called a "no brainer." Life has many such "spots" where you simply need to back off.

When the question parade marches through your mind, asking, "why am I not farther along; why haven't I reached the goal I set for myself a year ago," it is time to breathe and connect the dots: If everything you wanted to happen, happened up to this point, then you would have missed out on all the unexpected people and experiences you've encountered along *this* journey.

Where I thought I'd be in my life is a very different place than where I am presently, but as I look at all of my experiences, that I didn't plan, I see they were and are a right fit for me.

During my junior year of college, I decided to graduate early because I didn't like school. Expecting to dance professionally, I thought school was one giant bother. As I was standing in line to check out my books for the fall semester, I noticed a person in front of me holding a book titled, Native American Studies. Since I was a little girl, I had always been fascinated with Native American culture, so I inquired about the book. The person told me the book was for a Native American Cultural Anthropology class. I registered for the class and fell hook, line, and sinker for Anthropology and Archeology. I began to enjoy school and graduated with a minor in Anthropology.

When my Anthropology Professor heard I was moving to New York City, to dance, he called the Curator of the North American Archeology Lab at The American Museum of Natural History on my behalf. I was hired and worked, for over three years, as a pottery analyst in the North American Archeology Lab while launching my dance career. The job afforded me the opportunity to travel to St. Catherine's Island to work, where I met the program leader of an endangered sea turtle program. One summer, the program leader invited me along to help with the rescue and release of baby sea turtles. Releasing 101 baby sea turtles into the ocean, was quite an incredible experience, which was never in *my* plans.

Truly surrendering to the mindset of letting go of what you think you want and trusting in what is truly meant for you to experience, can open gateways to amazing opportunities! More times than not, life will deliver *BEYOND* your wildest dreams!

Relating to Surrender

Gentle Reminder: Surrender to Universal Order. Relax and enjoy the ride!

7
RELATING TO ROMANTIC RELATIONSHIPS

An authentic romantic relationship does not involve wanting to change your partner in any way. Instead, it respects and honors your partner's views, goals, and accomplishments. If change does occur, it is a personal choice and, hopefully, is perpetuated by a partner's positive influence.

You have a certain mission, dream, or goal to fulfill in this life that is yours alone. If a relationship is going to progress, you must be happy and feel complete in your "shoes." As two whole individuals, you can join together and build a solid partnership. You can walk similar paths, but not the same path.   Sharing mutual respect, love, and understanding, while supporting your loved one as you walk, "side by side" allows the relationship to be balanced, thus complimenting each person's dreams and goals.

When a relationship seems broken, like the heel on a shoe, you have to ask yourself, "can this be fixed?" Sometimes you put the shoe in the give-away bag, but then take it out. You try to fix the shoe and maybe it works and holds, or maybe, after a little more time passes, it breaks again.

Relating to Romantic Relationships

In romantic relationships, sometimes for you to move forward, you have to go back. There is no shame in this, nor is it a waste of time. It simply is part of the process. To be repetitive, for as long as it is necessary for you to learn your lesson, or in many cases, figure out your self worth, is okay. Going back can help you commit to your choices and change. This allows you to come to a new understanding with your partner or helps you see that your paths must diverge.

My first love was and still is an amazing man. After four years together, I began feeling my life shift in a different direction, away from the future I had originally planned with him. As new doors flew open for both of us, we began walking through them with different goals, and eventually our romantic relationship ended. After flying solo for a while, I began to get lonely and I started to question the decision we made to end the relationship. So, I called him and we got back together. It was good, but I realized, as did he, that we were better off as friends, which we still are to this day. Looking back, I see that it was in going back that I knew I must forge ahead.

Changing perception is often involved in moving forward. We can't invest all our hopes in another person to find our true happiness. It's only in finding our personal and unique happiness that we can fully have an authentic life experience. It is not about seeking out someone because you are alone or lonely. It is when you become comfortable enough to be alone with yourself that you can then make a conscious and clear decision to open your heart to another person and choose to share your life with him or her.

The first step toward finding that romantic right fit is honoring and valuing your *self*. You don't have to try and be someone you are not to appease or impress another person. It's like me trying to jimmy my bunion-bulging foot into a slender pair of extra narrow dress pumps. Trying to fit into what you think other people want rarely, if ever, works. Being less of who you are because you think it will make another person feel better is dishonoring both your *self* and your relationship. Free up closet space by discarding these old ideas and make room for new shoes, or in this case, a right relationship.

A while back, I went out on a few dates with a really nice guy who was shorter than I. I didn't care, but he continually commented on his height and how, at 5'8", I "towered" over him. I was dressing for our date and the pants I chose to wear looked spectacular with my favorite two-inch heels. I sat on the side of my bed and debated. Should I wear the heels or go out and buy a nice pair of flats for the date?

I wore the heels because I recognized I could not thwart my date's insecurities by lessening myself. This may seem like a simple example, but I feel the significance needs to be noted. Basically, I wasn't going to "lower" myself in order to encourage someone who was not valuing his own worth – or mine. If I had set that precedence, then something as minor as not wearing heels on our dates would have expanded to other changes, in order not to rock the proverbial boat. In the end, my date really liked my outfit, shoes and all, and our difference in height didn't seem to matter, since the entire evening was spent sitting in a theatre enjoying a musical.

Being in the right romantic relationship is not about being perfect or having yourself and your life all "figured out." In fact, it's the contrary. It is about having the awareness that you are cultivating yourself by understanding and acknowledging your strengths and weaknesses. It's about standing on your own two feet and at the same time being open and honest to your partner.

When you first find that right fit, it can be scary. If you are used to stuffing your feet into shoes that are too small, narrow, or stiff then finding that pair that seem to slide on so easily can seem too good to be true. At first, you may just assume the shoes fit you perfectly for the moment, but eventually will start to pinch. With that pinch, all your past relationships will come boiling up to the surface as you start to compare your past experiences with your current one. *STOP!* Releasing past relationships that didn't fit you and, in some cases, caused you pain, allows you to open your heart to that person and partnership you have been running a marathon to reach!

Put aside your fears, knowing the person in question has his or her own set of reservations and fears, too. Accept that even the most "perfect" pair of shoes has flaws, but you still want to wear them. Sometimes even that slight pinch at the beginning works itself out, never to be felt again.

So, pair up with your right fit and find your way together, one step at a time.

Gentle Reminder: With every relationship you evolve and excavate yourself into a deeper state of truth.

8
RELATING TO DISTRACTIONS

A distraction is anything or anyone that makes you take your eye off the mark. Making a breakthrough is part of the process of change and transformation. Setting a new course can be exciting and energizing. It is important to remember that people and situations will try to pull you off course.

Often, you focus your efforts and energy on other people and situations as an excuse not to focus on your own personal growth. It is much easier to shop for shoes, talk to a friend, clean, or reorganize your music collection than actually sit and do the work you have intended to do. On a deeper level, if the changes you are making are more emotional, it is easier to overeat, get involved in a relationship that is not benefiting you, or procrastinate to the point of falling behind with everyday obligations. You have all the shoes you need but keep shopping for more. Wear what you have and get movin'!

Not so long ago, I took a time-management test to see what my main focus was during the week. The shocking news was that it was cleaning. (No, I cannot come over to your house tonight with my Swiffer). Every time I sat down to work on a project, I would get distracted by some dust on a shelf or decide that I had to vacuum the carpet.

Relating to Distractions

Until I took this test, I had no idea I spent so much time tidying my house. With this new knowledge, I set a cleaning schedule. This helped tremendously. No longer would I allow myself to be distracted by a little spot on the carpet or a dust bunny under the bed. It would all wait until Saturday morning, which was my designated cleaning time.

When you are constantly focusing your attention on someone or something else, you are distracted from your goals. If you compare your attention to a light you carry to illuminate your path, you can surmise that if you are constantly shining that light on someone or something else, then you are left in the dark. It is very important to understand that it is not your job to carry the torch for everyone you care about throughout your lifetime.

Your job is to shine your light on yourself. When you find it challenging not to shine your light for the people you care about, keep in mind that this delays their progress. Growth through change sometimes requires a descent into the darkness. If you are constantly shining your light on a person who is in the midst of change, then he or she has no need to find their own light that will help them help themselves.

Take a moment and make a list of the things, situations, or people that may be distracting you from your progress. Make a pact, with yourself, to change by acknowledging what distracts you and finding a way to release it. Without distractions, you will find you will be able to keep your focus and accomplish your chosen goals more efficiently and joyfully!

Gentle Reminder: Focus on what makes you happy. By doing so, you will recognize what distracts you from your happiness.

9
RELATING TO HELPING OTHERS

In every relationship in your life, there will always be people you will feel compelled to help. I learned, through a series of trials and errors, if a person doesn't ask for help, you don't have the right to give it. When it comes to helping your friends, family, or even people you barely know, if they don't ask for help, you must step aside and let them figure it out on their own. This can be very difficult when you see someone you love going down the "wrong" path. Understand that everyone has a journey and it's that personal journey that leads to personal truth.

Small Shoes

Just like it is hard to control change in your life, it is a big *no, no,* to try and control the change in another person's life. By doing so, it's like making a person wear a pair of shoes *you* think look good on them. Interference, albeit with the right intentions, is not always the best option.

One day I was walking and came across a bee with tattered, worn out wings on the pavement. Feeling compelled to help, I picked up the bee from the sidewalk and placed her in a patch of flowers. The moment I set her down, a big hairy spider sprang from the flowers and captured her. I felt terrible. I had interfered and inadvertently the sweet little bee was eaten. It taught me a valuable lesson about trying to help others who are not asking for help: love them, pray for them, send them as much good energy as you possibly can, but let them "bee."

Gentle Reminder: If someone you know is in deep water, you can throw him or her a life raft (encouraging words, a hug, inspirational email), but it is his or her job to climb in and row to shore.

10
RELATING TO LIFE'S STEPPING STONES

Big, transformative changes can seem to happen in an instant. You finally move to your dream house, that perfect romantic relationship finds you, or you finally land that amazing job. In show business, this is called getting your big break, often followed by the phrase, "You're an overnight success!" When the big changes finally arrive, the transformation can seem like night turned to day.

All of a sudden you are wearing the fancy, high-end shoes from the exclusive boutique. Yet, remember all the other shoes that came before: the ones that helped you find your balance as a child, the ones that walked you through a difficult time, and the ones that gave you confidence during that big job interview.

Chances are a series of events or Stepping Stones were involved in getting you to the point where you are now standing. Positive or negative, Stepping Stones are there to help. They can reshape your life in ways you didn't think possible. Everyone who ever wronged you or helped you has gotten you to a new place, so thank them for being a Stepping Stone in your transformation.

I've experienced a multitude of Stepping Stones in my life through people and circumstances. In some cases, it has taken years to realize how a person or situation affected me and ultimately helped my growth.

Once, I attended a memorial service for an acquaintance that passed away. I went to show my respect to the family and friends of this person. They were some of the first people I met when I moved to Los Angeles. This entire network had taken me under their wings and showed me the way, literally and figuratively. After many years apart, I had forgotten what an amazing impact this network of people had had on my first few months in a new city. When I saw some of these people, some of whom I hadn't seen in over five years, a rush of emotions swept over me. It was like finding that old pair of beat up shoes in the back of the closet. They are the ones you'll never throw away because they carry so many memories in their "souls."

As my old friends and I laughed and cried about days past, I recognized how incredibly blessed I felt to know these people. Even though we'd gone our separate ways, in those few hours we were reunited, it was clearly apparent the times we'd spent together had impacted my life forever.

I have learned no matter how far you get in life, whether that means reaching all of your goals or not, there will always be a part of you that remains marked on each stone you have stepped upon. So, tread lightly with the awareness that you are a student and teacher on the path to your dreams. Acknowledge that a person or circumstance propelled you into a new phase of living and ultimately a new level of personal awareness.

Gentle Reminder: Be willing to accept every stepping stone that comes into your life. You can't possibly know where it will lead.

11
RELATING TO INDEPENDENT THINKING

In the words of the poet and dancer, Donlin Foreman,

We have to absorb influences

They are our building blocks

But our roots should be our own

At the base of all the learning and ideas

I have absorbed from others

I am

And must be

My own authority.

You can't always count on a specific person or thing to facilitate movement or be there to guide your steps. It's like the shoes in your closet that you wear more than most. Maybe they have actually molded around your foot. You rely on them because they compliment many outfits. But, what happens when those shoes wear out and you have to choose another pair?

I once had a friend who I depended on a great deal. Before making any major decision in my life, I sought this person's counsel. The advice given did resonate more times than not. Yet, by developing a dependency on this person, it hindered my own decision-making powers. When I was in a crisis and this person was absent, I didn't know where to turn. I had to rely on myself and that felt foreign. Prior to our friendship, I had always been an independent person. At least, I thought of myself as one, until I realized that I had stopped fully listening to myself and took my friend's word over my own. It was a bit of a struggle to disengage from this pattern and look inside myself for the answers, but it happened. The valuable lesson I learned was I didn't need anyone to validate or answer my questions for me, unless I wanted a second opinion.

Gentle Reminder: The first and most important opinion that you establish must be your own.

12
RELATING TO CHOICE

Conscious choice is a catalyst for change in any relationship. It's so easy to talk about something you want to do. The operative word is "do." When it comes to transitioning into something new, you must *DO* what you are talking about in order for your choice to induce change. Whether setting an intention like exercising every day or making a clean break from a relationship or job, if there is no energetic follow-through then it is a lot like looking at all of your shoes, but never wearing any of them.

Small Shoes

A man I knew once said, "We've all got 24 hours [in a day]." He was referring to people who make excuses why they can't do certain things because of seeming time constraints. When it comes to any form of change, procrastination and excuses can stifle progress. Tomorrow isn't another day. Today is *THE* day to get going on your dreams.

Choosing to do the necessary work to get to a place of learning, growing, and changing opens you up to a fantastic new menu from which you can place a new order for your life. At this stage of clarity, being specific about what you choose is key.

Relating to Choice

There's a wonderful online shoe store called Zappos.com. This site offers an endless array of shoes to choose from for any occasion. When a person goes to the site, he or she can type in the color, make, style, size, and even price of the shoes they are seeking. In life, you should "order" the same way by being specific about what you choose.

Want love? Make your order. Want a fulfilling career? Order it up! Want world peace? Now that's an order many should be placing…asap.

Making choices and placing your order requires you to mentally move forward. This usually entails restructuring old thought patterns or messages in your mind. When you delete "old messages," you are deleting the past. Just like you delete messages on your cell phone, you must delete messages of lack, delay, worry, and fear. There may be a continual effort, for some time, when it comes to deleting messages that are no longer serving the new you. By practicing positive choice, you'll soon do more saving than deleting. Then, only new messages of love, light, peace, and joy will steadily call to your consciousness.

Gentle Reminder: Make positive choices and remember Oprah Winfrey's words, "It is okay to change your mind."

13
RELATING TO YOUR THOUGHTS

You outgrow some of your shoes, just like you outgrow some of your thoughts. If a thought or thought pattern is no longer serving your highest good, toss it, just like you would a shoe that is too small or has gone out of style.

Sometimes a way of thinking becomes habit and mentally breaking away from the habit takes effort. It's like the space shuttle as it blasts off into space. The most treacherous and difficult part of its journey is breaking through the earth's barrier and gravitational pull. The shuttle shakes and rocks, as its boosters help catapult it to the stars.

Small Shoes

Practicing positive affirmations is one way to boost your thoughts into a new positive dimension. Affirmations can boost your energy and help you stay on the right track.

Not long ago, I made up my mind that I would like to change residences. At the time, a move didn't seem possible. I had few options, at least that I could see. Drawing from the teachings of Florence Scovel Shinn, I wrote the affirmation, "By Divine Right, my living situation improves immediately! I love where I live! This or something better!" After repeating this affirmation, daily, for several weeks, I put it away because I felt that I had said it enough.

Relating to Your Thoughts

I started to buy things for my new home that I loved. I tried seeing the beauty in my current living situation everyday, even though some days it was harder to see than others. Then, on my birthday, I decided to go to the beach for a walk.

Even though it was my birthday, I was not having the best day. A bit down, I thought a nice peaceful walk on the beach would do me good. As I descended the stairs leading to the open beach, I noticed a beached sea lion. I thought, *"Well, there goes my relaxing beach birthday."* Having volunteered for marine mammal rescue in the past, I knew I had to call someone about the seemingly sick sea lion.

After phoning the California Wildlife Center, I had to wait for the rescue team to arrive. During this time, I approached the handful of people on the beach and told them to stay away from the sea lion and that help was on the way. One man I spoke to took an interest in my marine mammal knowledge and we started to discuss various topics. At one point he asked where I lived and I told him. Then I asked him the same question. He told me he lived in a beautiful apartment on the ocean near a well-known meditation garden. I smiled and said I knew exactly where he lived, as I often visited the meditation garden and loved the area. Jokingly, I informed him that he'd better contact me if an apartment opened up in his building. He looked dumbfounded and said, "A vacancy sign was put up this morning."

Relating to Your Thoughts

On my way home from the beach, I passed by the building and there was the vacancy sign! Of course, my fingers couldn't fly across my cell phone fast enough. I scheduled an appointment to see the apartment the next day.

It was perfect. In fact, it was everything I had affirmed and more. I signed the lease and started to pack!

The "better" in my affirmation not only yielded an extraordinary apartment, but, an extraordinary low rent. To top it all off, as I was signing the lease, I thought how nice it would be to have an early move-in, as my schedule was filling up quickly. Sadly, it didn't seem possible. But, I decided to toss out that old negative thought and continued to think how nice it would be to move in early.

Out of the blue, the apartment manager called and told me the apartment was move-in ready and I could move in two weeks early, free of charge. So, after the perfect apartment found me, I also received two weeks, rent-free!

By the way, the sea lion survived and was released. ☺

Visualizing where you choose to be and saying daily affirmations is a part of "doing" the work. There is a lot to be said about positive energy and using it to surround your goals and dreams. By thinking positive, whatever you have to do instantly becomes easier.

Relating to Your Thoughts

This strength of will - literally willing the mind to think positive thoughts - breaks through the mind's gravitational pull. Memories and words of others may pull you back to thinking old thoughts but your heart knows the way. So, put on your space boots and know your own personal "boosters," or thoughts, can give you that final push, as you break away from old barriers and soar into your new life!

Gentle Reminder: Writing and repeating affirmations aloud impresses your conscious mind with the changes you wish to take place in your life. You must first be clear about what you choose: write it, say it, and feel it. Then, think positive! Engage in your life and be grateful for what you have and

Small Shoes

believe! Know that your affirmative thoughts will manifest at the right time, and could be even better than what you thought possible.

14
RELATING TO DOUBTS AND FEARS

Four ugly monsters that battle with change are: *Shoulda, Coulda, Woulda, and What If. Shoulda, Coulda, Woulda* and *What If* are all part of "The Doubt Family." The Doubt Family will always tell you you're not good enough, you should have done it this way, you could of said it that way, you would reach your goal if you were smarter or prettier...and on and on. Doubt can lock you into a mindset that shuts out any type of transformation.

At 15 years old, I was very impressionable. I was in high school and training at a hardcore dance academy. At school, I was constantly berated for being such a "goodie two shoes." A guy I liked told me he couldn't date me because I was "too tight laced." I would look at all the girls with boyfriends and think they were much more beautiful and popular than I. I struggled to fit in. At the dance academy, my instructors insisted that I was gaining weight, which was unacceptable to the program. Looking at my fellow dancers I would think they were better dancers, with better bodies and better skills.

The Doubt Family took up residence in my mind and heart. I was constantly comparing myself to others and had very little confidence in who I was and what I was contributing.

It took years for me to be happy with myself. Eventually, I spent more time with some very strong people, including two women I already knew, my Mom and Grandma. They helped me see my beauty and thus grow into the person I am today.

How do you keep those *dowdy* shoes out of your closet? You don't buy them. The same is true for The Doubt Family. To keep them out, don't buy into their lies and don't invite them in!

The Doubt Family wants to steal your confidence. If your thoughts and words turn negative, discouraged, and sad, so will the energy around you. This is food for The Doubt Family, and the more they eat, the stronger they become in your life.

Small Shoes

Thinking and speaking in a positive manner facilitates the highest form of change. If you are living in a joyful, positive vibration, you can't help but attract joyful, positive experiences. Even if your life is not exactly where you'd like it to be, if you wake every morning with a grateful, happy attitude, your day and the people and situations in it will support your progress.

There was a time when I was in a very challenging spot in my life. None of my relationships were a right fit and everything I was striving for wasn't coming to fruition. My acting career was stagnant, my living conditions were barely tolerable, and my boyfriend suddenly broke up with me. I was discouraged, negative, and extremely doubtful.

One day, I was talking to my Mom on the phone and she asked me the standard, "What's going on?" I heard myself reply, "Nothing new to report, same stuff, different day. I've really got nothing to say." All of a sudden, it hit me like a ton of bricks. How could my life change when I was constantly saying that everything was the same and that I had nothing to say? In that instant, I recognized I had allowed The Doubt Family to move in. I started saying, "I have a lot to say and wonderful news to report because my life is changing for the better!"

Within three months I booked a major acting job and within four months I moved into a beautiful new apartment. A surge of fantastic new people suddenly entered my life. I had served an eviction notice to the Doubt Family.

Put out doubt by saying, thinking, and feeling your worth and what you desire! Believe in yourself and watch for new beginnings!

Gentle Reminder: Keeping doubt out takes effort. Arm yourself with a strong support system, a healthy diet, and plenty of exercise.

15
RELATING TO DOING WHAT IT TAKES

We should never be told to do more. We should just do more automatically. We know all the steps. We sometimes just have a hard time putting them together to gain one flow, one movement. As long as you are moving, it's okay if you mess up the steps. The steps are there. You must put them altogether, and not stop - do not hesitate - not even for a second because it interrupts the flow. Just keep moving and you'll find that you are dancing!

-Alexander Tressor, Dance Instructor

Even if the dance steps seem difficult and the combination of your life impossible, it's okay. The key is to keep moving. Ballet slippers and Pointe shoes are designed to endure a lot of rehearsals and classes on the way to the opening night performance. Your mind, body, and spirit is designed to go the distance when you are learning, growing, and taking the necessary steps toward bettering your relationships.

Going the distance entails doing some things that may not exactly thrill you, but, by staying open to all possibilities and having the willingness to do what it takes to obtain your goals, you are often rewarded.

It's like wearing big bulky hiking boots. They may not look or feel great, but they will help you hike the steep canyon. When you reach the top, you are thankful you wore them, even if you cringed at the thought at first.

When I moved to Los Angeles to become a professional actor, I knew no one. I was a runner at a talent agency, which involved driving all over the city and dropping off packets of pictures to casting directors. Driving aimlessly around a foreign city is frustrating enough, but compound that with the fact that I was dropping off submissions for other actors, when I wasn't going on auditions, was hard to swallow. So, I decided to stop wallowing and volunteer for the Screen Actors Guild in the hopes of getting more involved in my acting career. My volunteer duties consisted of stuffing denim bags with leaflets, which was almost as bad as driving around town dropping off packets. I kept thinking, *"I went to college for THIS?"* Sticking with it, I was about two weeks into the project when my volunteer supervisor said he was forming a new department and needed a temporary assistant. It was a paid week and my job was to set up interviews to find a full time assistant.

At the end of the week, after the last interview had been conducted, the department head called me into his office and asked me if I would like to interview for the job. After all, we had been working together all week and it seemed like a good fit. The interview went well and he offered me the job, which I happily accepted.

For me, doing what it takes meant stuffing bags and being an assistant. The job gave me financial stability, networking opportunities, a flexible schedule, and invaluable life experiences, all of which positively influenced my acting career. By going the distance, I landed in a very good spot that supported my ultimate goal and my new lifestyle.

Gentle Reminder: Alexander also said, after giving a really hard dance combination, "It's going to be okay, I promise."

Thanks Alexander, you were and *are* right!

16
RELATING TO YOUR GIFTS

You have within you many unique treasures. How wonderful it is when you recognize your treasures and gift them to the world. Never underestimate your strength and ability to spread joy and happiness.

Your relationship to your gifts can bridge relationships throughout the world and initiate change. A smile, a caring word, a random act of kindness can set the tone for a better day, a better year, and a better life. Something as "small" as telling a stranger that they look pretty or putting a quarter in a parking meter that is about to expire can have a significant positive ripple effect.

Sometimes the stress of life can bury your treasured gifts. You get so busy that you keep tossing all of your shoes in your closet, only to discover, months later, that a treasured pair, have been sitting at the bottom of the heap. As in life, you must keep acknowledging your gifts and not let them get tossed aside.

Maybe your treasure chest is buried under mounds of dirt. Maybe you need a map to find it. Sometimes, it takes a certain relationship to help you recognize or redis-cover your gifts. It's as simple as a friend shopping with you and pointing out a pair of shoes you wouldn't necessarily buy on your own. These shoes may reflect a part of you that you have been hiding away that your friend can see and nudges you to address.

By relating to and honoring your gifts, you can unearth your contribution to the world.

Gentle Reminder: Take a moment and think about the people in your life and the experiences you hold close. Find the treasure in your accomplishments and seeming failures.

17
RELATING TO FAMILY AND FRIENDS

Friends and family can be interchangeable. Some of your friends may seem more like family and some of your family members may seem like distant friends, if not mere acquaintances. Some family members, like some shoes, can be worn only for short periods of time, and some friends, like your really comfortable shoes, can be worn all the time.

The fact is you don't have to share DNA with someone to call him or her family. How you relate to your family or your friends that feel like family depends on the circumstance. You've been influenced and shaped by your upbringing and sometimes the actions and opinions of your family are not in alignment with your adult choices, whereas your friends are in alignment with your choices. Sometimes family members simply can't be there for you and it is a friend that steps up.

During my childhood, it was my family that bore my strongest relationships and I count myself as one of the lucky ones to have had that solid foundation. My mother and father allowed me to soar out of the nest at a very early age so I could pursue my passion for dance, and, quite literally, helped me put on my ballet shoes.

Relating to Family and Friends

In my early twenties, the family members I was closest to, including my grandparents, Sam and Carmel, aunts and uncle, Norma, Carmel and Ralph, neighbors, Rose and Sam, family friends, Laura, Benny, and Richard all passed away within three years of each other. I went from a packed Thanksgiving Day dinner table to my Mom, Dad and me. It was a huge adjustment because I relied on those relationships with my family. Eventually, a handful of friends entered my life and they soon became family. Many of these friends, if not all, were right fits from the start. When I met one of my closest girlfriends, she ironically helped me fill my closet with great shoes. And when my father was gravely ill, she hopped on a plane, abandoning her busy life, and was by my side. How could I call her anything less than family (thanks Jules ☺). I'm also blessed to call other really spectacular people I've met family, and have many sisters and a few brothers living all over the world.

Friends and family contribute to your life in their own unique way. Stay open to meeting new family members throughout your life and appreciate those you have in your life right now. Like some of your shoes, you don't always have to like them, but show love for them because they have had a part in helping you step in the right direction.

Relating to Family and Friends

Gentle Reminder: Extend the branches of your family tree out to the friends you hold close to your heart.

18
RELATING TO TRUST
& PATIENCE

In all of your relationships, there has to be an element of trust and patience. Trusting that a pair of running shoes will get you to the finish line of a marathon can be a lot easier than trusting a certain person or situation will come through for you. Being patient when breaking in new shoes seems simpler than being patient when you are waiting to hear about a job interview or a second date.

Trust and patience is essential when you decide to change any relationship. I think this is especially evident when you are changing jobs or moving from one location to another. As you choose to transform your lifestyle, situations and people will sometimes try to hold you back. You may feel uncertain. You may become impatient. You may want to give up. This is when it is crucial to trust and be patient.

When it comes to trust and patience, I depend on animals to be my guide. Baby sea turtles are great teachers. I've had the opportunity to work with these tiny creatures and each time I do, they remind me to trust in myself and to have patience in life's process. They also have taught me to never give up.

Relating to Trust & Patience

Weighing no more than 25 grams, baby sea turtles emerge from their nests on the beach, at night, and trek to the ocean. Change is almost instantaneous as the ocean air turns their soft shells hard and the secure warm nest they shared with their clutch mates is abandoned for a twenty- mile swim, alone. The turtles often reach the surf only to be battered back to shore. Again they try with great fortitude to surmount the waves until they reach the open ocean. Once in open ocean, they swim steadily, taking paced breaths along the way, until they reach a chain of seaweed that serves not only as shelter, but as a type of vessel that helps transport them home to a chain of small islands.

I imagine turtles saying, *"We are small, yet have all of the support and guidance we need within us to face the challenging swim ahead. As we make our way into the water, the beach is dark and sometimes it's hard for us to see what is ahead. This is when we must trust. The waves sometimes take us back to shore, just when we thought we were over them, and sometimes we even get turned around in the wrong direction!*

Eventually, we master the waves and reach the open ocean. There, we know we must pace ourselves, coming up for air, folding our tiny flippers on our shells to rest. We must have patience. It is a long swim for such a little body, but we do not focus on our size. Instead we focus on the task at hand and swim forward into our future.

Relating to Trust & Patience

It is time to focus on your future. Whatever relationships are changing in your life, have trust and patience, align with your inner power, and through darkness and waves, forge ahead!

Gentle Reminder: "Nature does not hurry, yet everything is accomplished." Lao Tzu

19
RELATING TO DISAPPOINTMENT AND HOPE

What right do you have to be exempt from joy? In a society full of wants, needs, and goals, when you fall short you feel disappointed. Sometimes, it's quite warranted, and certainly is a part of the process of change.

Being a professional actor, I audition for various roles, many of which I do not book. I usually have to vent my disappointment, sometimes cry, before I can accept the job was not mine. By acknowledging my true feelings, I allow myself to come to a place of peace.

Small Shoes

Sometimes you stick to lower emotions, even liking or reveling in them to a degree. You look for reasons to complain, to pity, or to stay stagnant and "safe." It's like wearing an old pair of worn out smelly shoes. They might be familiar, but are they warding off new opportunities?

As you go into any new relationship, isn't it easier to assume the worst and prepare for rejection? By preparing for the worst, you shield yourself from any pain that might be caused if you had anticipated a situation with high hopes. If things don't work out with that new lover, job, housing bid, you won't feel so disappointed.

Why not strive for the best all the time? Why not have high hopes? Allow yourself the joy of dreaming. Sure, things don't always work the way you would like them to, but if you are brave enough to be still, and really look at a situation that you had chalked up as a failure, ten times out of ten, you will find that what you didn't receive allowed you the opportunity for a more perfect circumstance.

Gentle Reminder: Be ready and prepared. Then, let it all go. Whatever happens will be the right fit for you.

20
THE RIGHT FIT

We are all connected in this constant changing world. We get distracted and tied up in our own thoughts and relationships. By freeing the mind and opening the heart, clarity has a path to proceed.

The constant cycle of life allows you to encounter new relationships with people and situations. Some will stay with you and others will be outgrown. All will enrich you in some way.

The only thing you have to do is be yourself. Embrace who you are and love your *self*!

Small Shoes

Who and what is meant to be in your life will be in your life.

Think about how much baggage you carry because you are not true to yourself and your real desires. If you have worn penny loafers all your life, but really like more flashy footwear, break out and get some leopard print flats! Reinventing yourself is a fantastic catalyst to authentic change and inevitably will lead you to all the right fits in every style, shape, and size.

Where will you be tomorrow? Where will you be five minutes from now? How will these moments change you? As overwhelming as these questions may be, they only steal from the moment you are living now. *LIVE.* Be in Joy.

Change, whether voluntary or mandated, can lead to a transformation of Self. To transform is to choose to change and be open and aware of shifting perceptions and new waters. Understand that you are not dependent on any one person or situation for anything because you possess all the support, all the joy, and all the love you need within yourself. This type of resolve gives you freedom to choose new paths and new adventures!

Small Shoes

You now possess a new perspective. The drama, patterns, and worn out situations of your old life are released and there are no hidden constraints holding you back. A new relationship, a new job, a new home, a new friendship, a new romantic partner, or a new state of mind, finds you, just like a perfect pair of shoes that slide on so easily.

They are made just for you.

It's the right fit.

At last.

GENTLE REMINDER EXERCISE

BREATHE

With each breath you begin again. Each breath can change the way you feel. If you find yourself in a high stress situation, stop and breathe. If you need to focus your energy, stop and breathe. If you are nervous, anxious, or even excited, stop and breathe.

Breathe. Go ahead. Take a great big deep breath right now.

Again.

Once more.

Good.

How do you feel? Check in with your body.

Where are your shoulders? Are they up around your ears, or are they relaxed and in alignment with your back?
Roll your shoulders back and allow them to "fall."

Breathe.

How is your jaw? Is it locked?

Open your mouth really really wide (I know you feel silly, but this will help, promise). Stretch out your jaw. Now relax your mouth and let your jaw relax. If your mouth

Gentle Reminder Exercise

is slightly hanging open, you are doing this exercise correctly.

Breathe.

Check in with your tongue. Is it plastered on the roof of your mouth? Let your tongue "fall" and relax.

Breathe.

Roll your neck one direction, then the other.
Breathe.
Roll your wrists one direction, then the other.
Breathe.
Take off your shoes, and roll your ankles.
Breathe.

Small Shoes

Now, shake your entire body! Let it all hang out!   Make noise.

Dance around. Jump up and down!

      Breathe. Breathe. Breathe.

Settle.

      Breathe.

Close your eyes AFTER you read the following:

Open your mind and heart. Visualize blue skies, green meadows, colorful flowers, snow brushed mountains, rainbows, and anything else that brings you peace.   When this feels complete, open your eyes.

Now, close your eyes and begin.

GENTLE REMINDERS

Gentle Reminder: As you are developing your relationships, are you planning, pushing, and forcing? Or, are you setting an intention with faith that it will work out in your favor? Plans equal pressure. Plans offer little movement. Instead of planning, simply set intentions. There is fluidity in intentions. Intentions can morph and change, allowing any relationship to breathe and grow.

Gentle Reminder: When you race up the mountain, you may fall. But if you take steady steps, one step at a time, you'll make it to the top.

Gentle Reminder: Communication is the key. Speak your truth with integrity and compassion.

Small Shoes

Gentle Reminder: If something scares you, do it anyway. You'll start to gain momentum against fear and you'll be fueled by faith!

Gentle Reminder: Sometimes the shoes you wear have to take you far, so be smart about what you choose. Learn how to balance your responsibilities and intentions. If you feel rushed or overburdened, try a different pace.

Gentle Reminder: There are times in life when you are in panic mode. Stop pushing and breathe... Accept what is happening in the moment.

Gentle Reminder: Forgiveness is very powerful. You don't have to forgive the action, but forgive the person. In doing so, you are leaving room for positive change.

Gentle Reminders

Gentle Reminder: Stop asking what everything means. Just know that you are a strong person and have to wait sometimes for life to catch up with you.

Gentle Reminder: If you are stressed or facing a big decision, spend time outside, rain or shine. Nature heals and is very grounding.

Gentle Reminder: The Universe sends you curve balls. Have confidence and be ready to hit 'em outta the ballpark!

ABOUT THE AUTHOR

Camille was born in Ashtabula, Ohio. At an early age, she became enthralled with dance and musical theatre and dedicated most of her childhood to dance classes, rehearsals, and performances. At age 15, she moved from her home in Ashtabula, to Mayfield, Ohio, to study with The School of Cleveland Ballet. She graduated from Mayfield High School and continued her education at Mercyhurst College, in Erie, Pa., earning a degree in Dance and Anthropology. Camille's next move was to New York City where she studied and performed with The Martha Graham Dance Company and worked as a pottery analyst for The American Museum of Natural History.

Small Shoes

Always in tune with change, Camille shifted her focus from dance to acting, and performed with The Shakespeare Theatre in Washington DC, before making the coastal leap to Los Angeles, CA, where she presently resides, and is a professional actress. Along with acting, Camille is pursuing screenwriting and producing, and is currently working on a film project to raise awareness for the endangered African Elephant.

Passionate about conservation and animals, Camille has journeyed to Borneo, Indonesia to film and study the endangered orangutan and has worked with an endangered sea turtle program, along the Georgia Coast. She volunteers at The California Wildlife Center and is a Working Student at The Traditional Equitation School.

About the Author

To Camille, a day well spent is a day with family and friends (pet companions included), or a day at the barn, horseback riding, or a day of snapping photos of sweeping vistas, while hiking canyons along the California Coast.

Camille Licate

SmallShoesthebook@gmail.com

www.camillelicate.com

Made in the USA
Charleston, SC
19 February 2012